The French Exit

THE FRENCH EXIT

Poems by Elisa Gabbert

BIRDS, LLC | AUSTIN, MINNEAPOLIS, NEW YORK, RALEIGH

Birds, LLC
Austin, Minneapolis, New York, Raleigh
www.birdsllc.com

Design by M. Joshua Elliott
Edited by Sampson Starkweather

Library of Congress Cataloging-in-Publication Data:
Gabbert, Elisa
The French Exit/Elisa Gabbert
Library of Congress Control Number: 2010901310

First edition, 2010.
ISBN-13: 978-0-9826177-1-7
Printed in Canada

Acknowledgements

Thanks to the editors of the journals where some of these poems (sometimes in earlier versions) originally appeared: *42opus, Anti-, Area Sneaks, Boog City, Cannibal, Coconut, Colorado Review, Diagram, H_NGM_N, Kulture Vulture, The Laurel Review, LIT, Melancholia's Tremulous Dreadlocks, Meridian, No Tell Motel, The Raleigh Quarterly, RealPoetik, Redivider, Salt Hill,* and *Typo.*

"No New Years Just Higher Numbers" appeared on a limited-edition broadside created by Catherine Bourassa-Hebert.

"The Dream Because Love Ends" was republished in *The Bedside Guide to No Tell Motel – Second Floor.*

A number of these poems also appeared in the chapbooks *Thanks for Sending the Engine* and *My Fear of X* from Kitchen Press.

For love, friendship, and help with the creation of this book, I'd like to thank my parents; John Cotter; my editors: Dan Boehl, Justin Marks, Matt Rasmussen, Chris Tonelli, and especially Sampson Starkweather; Josh Elliott; Caroline Knox, Noelle Kocot, and Kevin Prufer; Kathleen Rooney and Martin Seay; Simeon Berry; and Paige Taggart.

Contents

III.

COMMISSIONED

It starts here, where you begin
remembering. (How else could it begin?)

You find a notebook, the first several pages
filled in with your own writing, red pen.

You must know what it says.
But in the dream you can't read it.

In dreams there's no quality to the weather.
But an orange sky, hanging. Something it means.

You can't much feel. What you would smell—
your ash breath in the air—is translated elsewhere,

absorbed into the visual field.
So the landscape pulsates,

supersaturated with meanings.
With meaning*ness*.

Things that are orange.
Things that sting.

That trill. That signal possession.
Dissipate. Are marred.

You kick a car, and it crumples apart
like a death-hollowed tree.

"Pain" ripples out in a wave.

I.

WHAT HAPPENED

It looks sweet there, concussed.

Then the body wakes up.

Extracts itself from a hood of blood—

Shakes off its addenda, composites—

Sleeves of glass—

It rises—It stands in her outline

Like a mouthed word—

Exquisite—Or *glister*—Or *lust*.

It moves toward the bathroom.

Looks in the mirror

To find out what happened.

Nobody sees this.

She doesn't know.

Broke. Or *syncope*.

Or *glow*.

X

Mindless, the body is perfect,

an outline—form without
content, absent of tone, lying

in the street. Faint halo of white
where it touches the concrete.

When a car almost hits you
you actually scream; it's embarrassing.

Unless you die instantly.
In the best of all possible worlds

you die instantly, before
the formation of memory, scars.

Before there were stop signs.
Before there were cars.

I want to lie on the top level
of an empty garage, to be close

to the sky as I lose my mind—
I'm afraid. I'm afraid

I'll feel pretty
transcendent.

POEM WITH A THRESHOLD

In the grip of the NYC sublime
I fell in love out of boredom.

I left the party, through the French exit
to the smaller one inside

where the cake said
I HAVE NO CONCEPT OF TIME.

Look into my image
distortion disorder and tell me

what you really feel, now
that you're incomprehensible, Mr.—

tell me "what for." I love you
but my arms are full.

I opened my face with the door.

CAMERA OBSCURA

Candelabra on the wainscoting, hairline fracture
on the ceiling. An ancient stereopticon

leaves dust rings around my eyes. This tiny room
cannot contain my desire. My desire

flaps and beats against the walls
like an idiot bird trapped inside the flue.

The pinprick of light could be coming
from any direction. Somewhere else

the sky withholds its endlessness. On the tip
of my desire's tongue—flame blue.

Desire explodes and the last thing it feels
is every point touching something.

DAY TRIP WITH SPIRES

We enter the cathedral. I fall for it every time,
gothic trick of the mind—awe, guilt, fear of X, all of it—

made small by this capaciousness, destroyable. Inside
I'm sort of clicking, trying to engage, but behind that

more of me is lost, in a fugue. The illogic
of cathedrals—we're mostly empty space anyway—

I don't want to apprehend the unknown.
When I'm crying I remember how as a child

I always thought someone was watching me.
This was my earliest sense of the erotic.

I GET EMOTIVE ON PLANES

A stab of joy during the movie, or simple pain—
I cried. The ignoble cry of the anonymous

passenger. It's not a scene if everyone ignores it,
my quivering eye. Self-sabotage, at this point,

would be suicide. X-ray outline of somebody's penknife—
I saw a picture of John's hand on the back of my head.

Always in joy I am parallel to a suffering
"out there," a bad front. When I said,

The clouds feel like nothing when you're in them,
he said, *No, they feel like frozen fog*—

confusing feeling with seeming, I think.
And nothing, and suffering, with fog.

MUST-SEE MOVIE

It goes backwards, starting in the oubliette—
the end of my life as we know it—
and then I'm tumbling up the rabbit hole.

Hair billowing out like I'm underwater.
The Seven Sisters in the distance.
The Well-Tempered Clavier in reverse.

The man who pushed me pulls me up,
embraces me. We enter a room
by way of the exit. It's an inquiry

into causation: Why do my clothes
smell of poppies? Why am I splayed
in the field? It's windy now—was it calm

this afternoon? Did the skies imply rain,
just before they blurted it out?
Pan to the periphery—here is the car

that I dreamily lock myself out of.
Here is the lot where I'm stunned by
the illusion of choice. We meet the family,

watch my brother eat the meat
he just spat out; my mother at her loom,
unweaving all morning. Now I'm gliding,

winding through the house,
up the stairs: face-forward to the camera,
face pale and blank. The tension

builds, the soundtrack crescendos,
as I undress, the final bright revealing—
then fall uncontrollably back to sleep.

I EVEN FEEL TIRED IN MY DREAMS

I have to finish the tennis match but just want to sleep.
Small dogs leap up and latch onto my arms.

I want to lie down, let them have me.
But if I die before my mom she'll never forgive me.

I can see my pulse pounding right through the skin.
How minor can a heart attack be?

Can you have one in your sleep and not die or even start?
Just sleep right through it like a too-soft alarm? *ee ee ee* ...

I often smoke in my dreams. Am a dancer. Eat meat.

Every heartbeat is a minor attack. How many blips
make an army? Tiny brute-hearted army.

The faster your metabolism, the shorter your life span.
I'm down there with lab mice. I empathize completely.

Concordance: "right through." As in a trapdoor.
My mom is going to die. The word *lupus* means "wolf."

Most commonly named wish that is also a fear:
to die in one's sleep.

AUBADE

We both dream about wild animals.
There had been a dog fight at the party—

the older, bigger dog somehow threatened
by the puppy, a girl—he was chasing her

in circles around the yard, knocking over drinks
and gnawing on her leg. I tensed

when they bumped against mine.
You said not to be afraid of them,

they're only dogs. A rash prickled up there
and I scratched it all night.

The birds screech outside at this bleak hour.
Why do they always sound terrorized?

It's a wave—their cries, the encroaching light;
the room growing paler in pindots,

coming up to our edges. Us feeling separate.
The nightmare you gave me, or caught.

POEM WITH INTRINSIC MUSIC

Empty tennis courts of autumn,
the landscape wants to appropriate you

like fallow cortex, the brain over-
turning itself: A blind woman has no use

for sports, but the cells could go
to memorizing Bach—the cello suites,

the overtures. This one's like tipping
your head back to take in the sky gone

shallow, dimensionless—shot
with no timestamp, the rule of threes.

Seesaw, seesaw. One is like dust.
Cricket legs/wings. Another: approaching

the treeline to find they're not far
away, just very small trees.

POEM WITH ATTEMPTED SUICIDE
AND/OR AUTOEROTIC ASPHYXIATION

When the boredom hits,
I hit the boredom

like a glass door. Oh my god,
what am I for? I would throw

a game of solitaire;
I would throw myself

off the trail.
But for the railing,

I'm this close
to deforestation porn—

the trees aground,
all around my hole self,

the blasted air. I'd jump in
if I could let go.

I can defenestrate anything
except for the window.

DECOHERENCE

In my sex-dream-cum-anxiety-dream
my ex decides at the last minute
he's not interested in giving me another chance—

my current bedroom, where he's never been.
The light black & blue like night on film.
A dream of the future, blurring the past.

Fear of Missing Out or Fear of Not Knowing?
Variations on the same theme.
He was doing this quantum thing

every time I looked away—
half in the bed and half leaving.
Knowing I'd revert to my one-note innocence.

I keep thinking about a woman I met.
One day, approaching an intersection,
she was afraid she wouldn't be able to stop walking.

POEM WITH VARIATION ON A LINE
FROM *SATURDAY NIGHT FEVER*

I want anterograde timelessness:
I want to invent the future,

so people will think I came from it,
sent back to the present–as–past.

My desires depend on their being
pent, unrealized. My desires are unreal

in the future's eyes. Like knives.
The whole point of a stab wound

is the poignant memory. I don't invent
the future; the future invents me.

And then forgets me.

POEM WITH A SUPERPOWER

Exquisite me. Angelic me.
I never say I'm sorry for anything

(one of us thinks). I can't remember
the present, for all the unthinkable

future reversing back into me.
Tentative. Me in suspense.

The art on the walls is hanged
at nefarious angles;

a boy at the counter disappears,
or I can see through him.

How does my X-ray vision
know when to stop? I

was trying to get to the way end.

THE DREAM BECAUSE LOVE ENDS

The person I'm playing tennis with keeps changing
back and forth between my brother and my ex-boyfriend—

I hope this means nothing; I just miss them both;
they make me feel fucking horrible. Some part of me knows

it's 4 a.m. and I'm too weak to dive for a shot; my racket strings
are on the verge of snapping gloriously like Achilles' tendons.

Allen wears the face from when we went apt. hunting
and he called all the places in our price range Calcutta.

As soon as I think of that flying roaches enter from the west.
My brother whacks at them with his old Wilson

as they whiz by our ears at their disgusting frequencies,
skating black figure 8's against the dusty sky.

We make a run for the Pro Shop and soon enough
we're drinking orange soda on the couch like everything is OK;

Allen drapes one of his long arms, his Hong-Kong-brown arms,
piano-hand arms, road-hockey-scarred-elbow arms

across my shoulder and says that everything is OK. On TV
they're showing footage from the courts and it seems like

we're still out there: Man vs. Nature. I wonder out loud
if it's some kind of joke and one of them says *If it is,*

it's the saddest, the longest, the slowest, most beautiful joke
you could tell. He doubles me over. He knows me so well.

II.

BLOGPOEM FOR APRIL

You can't invent a color, only name it,
like how I just named those contrails Benjamin
and then the sky behind them Benjamin II.
Now, retronymically, I refer to Ben as Ben I.
If he becomes famous, they'll stop calling
clouds "clouds" and call them "nonlinear
clouds" or "pre-Benjamin" for clarity.
I can think about fame all day, and
compose apologies for my friends' friends
who I've variously snubbed, write them
into emails with personalized P.S.'s:
P.S. My love for you extends forever
in all directions, or sometimes seems to.
P.S. I include a swatch of Yves Klein blue.
P.S. If the sky is a piano store and clouds
are baby grands, we just hang out in the back
and listen to a Casiotone's preprogrammeds.
P.S. This P.S. is my email's last will
and testament. It's leaving everything
to you. P.S. Like my love for you,
like the infinite crystalline watchface of
God of the sky, my email will never die.

ORNITHOLOGICAL BLOGPOEM

You will be woken by the chirping of the birds, which is the sound
of their egos escaping from their bodies in loud and irregular streams.
They are acupuncture birds; where the chirps fall on your eardrums
corresponds to where you experience the pain. The birds have PhDs.
They chirp out chapters from their dissertations. The birds do not agree
that irony is dead. One of the birds has tried repeatedly to fall to its death
but always starts flying at the last second. The birds are excessively
vain about their wings. They have been known to assemble themselves
into bridges and other structures. An obelisk of feathers. Do not feed
the birds; they are following a strict high-protein diet. The birds are
control freaks. Do not, under any circumstances, try to touch their beaks.
One of the birds has assumed a leadership role. Another bird is plotting
to assassinate it. Some items have gone missing from the kitchen. The
birds are capable of eating almost anything but are far too discriminating.
If you are lucky one morning the birds may chirp selections from your
favorite opera. The birds are especially fond of Wagner. What would you
like to hear? They have a very long waiting list and are nepotistic. Do not
be afraid of angering the birds. What angers the birds is fear.

BLOGPOEM FOR JOE

He's your first friend named Joe: funny, isn't it?
With a name like Joe, it seems as though
you should have met him before. He reminds you
of someone, he will always remind you
of the first Joe, because he is. It makes you feel
warm, but then you start to wonder if it's him
you like or just the name—but you can't
go smoke on the deck with the name Joe,
can't take it to a show. You can't get a call
from the name Joe, though until you pick it up
it kind of looks that way. You can, I guess,
write a poem about the name, but the name
can't read it. Or won't. No, you decide,
it's Joe: this Joe and not the idea-of-Joe,
the meaning-of-Joe, not the concept
but the instance, the example of Joe (e.g.,
Joe). It's like you just took a bite of
the most perfect peach in all of Venice,
and now you never want a peach again. You
want this one to be the last you'll ever know.

BLOGPOEM W/ ELLIPSES

. . . fixed my car. Kind of
miss the dent, when I see
the anti-hole where it used
to be. Where do holes go
to die? Their cemetery
sure would seem a waste
of space—all those graves
of graves. Can't throw
any of the dirt back in
without crushing the holes
to another death. So no one
can mourn them again. . . .
I've started practicing
creative apathy. Can't
spend all day in transit
among various funerals.
Everybody's got the
same epitaph anyway:
Was Alive. Is Not. Tried
To Save Life Thru Not
Caring. Died Bored.

BLGPM W/ DTHWSH

Take me to the library; I'm in the mood
to get murdered. Mmm, murder in the stacks:
shove the LING shelving over and let those
uncracked grammars in teal and burnt umber
make papery work of the burying. Chris,
this is me courting depression, or it courting
me. I'm not seduced by death, just death's
techniques—the way it lets me let it buy me
a drink. Then drives me home w/ the lights off,
in stealth mode. I want that void *in* me.
Speed-reading the convoluted passages
at my left brain's innermost vortices.
We vector cliffward, we pin the needle
like there's nothing more to lose than
this week's top score on Pole Position.
Fuck you, existence: I'm playing to win.

BLOGPOEM W/ BLUE BALLS

Dude. How could you seduce me w/
your date-rape-drug metaphor, your
beautiful, your bisexual non sequitur,
& then make like a tree for the neon
SORTIE sign of our moment's theater?
You missed a great scene: the fields
on screen just exploded into lushness
like contagious brushfire, like they'd
nabbed a horrifically gorgeous rash.
Now the moment's over; can't even
save the stubs 'cause the tix've been
digitized. But it's all in my mind—
your bloodshot, your gut-shot eyes,
your phraseology all sibilant & slant-
rhymed like a pseudo-sonnet from
the Portuguese. DUDE. Your sweat
Chinese-water-tortures me, you make
my heart feel like a would-be Houdini,
etc.

BLOGPOEM AS MEME, OR
BLOGPOEM AFTER DANIEL DENNETT

If it really wanted to get through to you
this poem would do better as an ant virus,
with DNA designed to make the ant think
I've fucking got to climb that grass blade,
thereby facilitating its being eaten by
a grazing cow. Because the virus wants
to be inside the cow. Or thinks it does—
but actually it's my virus in the virus
that makes it think that. My virus
is waiting for you to eat the cow.
That would be a great poem, because
while it was doing that I could,
you know, have a beer, or work on
my frittata skills, or write the virus poem
instead of the poem about it.

BLOGPOEM W/ AUTORAPE

There are no new words, words I haven't mis-
pronounced or -used before, so I'm starting over—
with that A-hole who gave me an Atomic Harvest
tape and his debate club shirt that said
Making the world safe for hypocrisy; he saw
all those kids get killed in the bonfire, left a creepy
note on my car that I balled up and tossed
in the dumpster. I was eating an eggplant
parmesan sub, I lost that too. This is my fake
abecedarian, blasphemous chiclet diary entry
read by no one. Feels like getting caught
telling jokes to myself that I've already heard.
They pretty much tell themselves, I pretty much
just sync them up with my laugh track. I'd like
masturbation better if it could be a surprise attack.

BLOGPOEMS ARE IDEAS

Time capsules are so retro I want to send one back
into the past, with a note on each item of kitsch—
some popular snack package or a poignant hat—
that says *Totally you*, or *You go like this*. Maybe
I could fool the reverse-archaeologists into thinking
I'm their future king. People were stupider then,
less evolved than us because they didn't have to learn
how to overcome cancer or master the joystick.
They had simple concerns that didn't require calculus
or metaphysics, like ridding mice from the pantry
and putting out occasional house fires. And yet,
as far as we've come, technology still lags behind
our desires. For instance science hasn't solved
the problem of weather: how much of it there is,
and how it is literally everywhere.

BLOGPOEM THE LITANY

It wasn't really flying. More like a breeze
stiff enough to blow me with my toes
just dragging thru the tulip fields. The tulips
need cross-kingdom interaction. The bees
need a day off. Amsterdam needs a Richter
scale of quaintness. The museums need
hyperlinks. The clouds need a comment box.
The insects need a revolution, the bridges
need mnemonics, the canals need lucid
dreams. They need to read the memoirs
of a river. Staff pick: the Ganges'. The kids
need more advanced diversions, they need
a hovering trike: Hummingbird™. Society
needs more tulips, yet more—the fields
are wide. The people need more opiates, or less.
One way or the other they are not satisfied.

LOUSY DAY BLOGPOEM

Was the end of a lousy day. Drank too much
and everyone agreed my emotions were implausible.
Once again I couldn't prove the theorem,
once again I had no love for anyone or vice versa
(anyone had no love for me). There was no art
on the train and then it never came, made me late
for my appointment with the firing squad,
my last disappointment. Day was a wash
but its poem was a sidekick that tried to cheer
it up. The day rode along mostly lost in thought
and the traffic had died out for the most part
and the poem was the day's faithful sidecar.
Stuck around to listen to the fusillade.

DISASTERPOEM (FOR KR)

I want to drive under the overpass all night,
turn the stripe of light, the light's blink
to a strobe effect—turn the light epileptic—

the interior goes orange, night-orange, the orange
of black—the edges go sharp/slack, sharp/
slack. I think *So this is how it feels to be high*—

I always think that when I'm high . . .
and I play and replay the film clip of K
when she stood up to go—when the towering

wave of her drunkenness hit, flattened her
there—when she fell like a building
down into itself, its own empty air—

freeze frame and rewind—those heart-breaking
legs, collapsible spires—it never gets old.
She's with me now, half-asleep in the back

and ice-cold and now the moths are coming,
the moths of spring—moving toward the car
as it moves toward them—we will pass

through each other's fields. Don't be afraid, K—
though afterward we may not remember
who we were before the crash.

RENAISSANCE BLOGPOEM

Already today's sky is replacing
yesterday's sky in my mind.

It, like all skies, was an unforgettable
sky, but nonetheless I'm starting

to forget it, as the sky comes cresting over
yesterday's horizon like a monster wave—

as it comes scrolling upward like
film credits to tell us our new names—

I can't rewind or skip back to my fave
scenes, of one wing flapping,

one-half of a white horse galloping. . . .

★

Like a lesser Michelangelo

my poem had inessential parts
so I rolled it down a great hill and

they broke off. Now my poem is a sphere
I hold in my palm—it's the size

of a spider's eye. I cast it out
into the wind. I know tomorrow

the wind will blow me another one.

BLOGPOEM AFTER WALTER BENJAMIN

Every time you reproduce a piece of art
you remove some of its aura and that's why
your mix tape didn't impress me much,
it was so fucking aura-less
                                      but in the film
version of the novelization of this poem
I play myself but have fantastic breasts
and there are probably some blood baths

and also when my fangy tooth catches
on my lip men everywhere crumple
w/ the ecstasy and agony of it and really

who needs aura in your movie when
you're so hot it breaks people's knees.

BLOGPOEM@SEA

When I was trapped on the island
I had plenty of time to read but nothing to read
except what I spelled out myself
in shells on the beach, my daily blog entry.
I did a lot of writing on the island
but eventually forgot how to read.
I finally learned to dance but learned I hate dancing.
I constantly thought I heard a phone ringing.
Or a microwave dinging.
I named my favorite trees and my least favorite trees.
Over time they all became my least favorite trees.
I often stared at my feet and hands.
I stared at fish bones and grains of sand.
I stared so long at the sky I went partially blind.
The clouds were shaped like things I'd never seen,
things that hadn't been invented yet.
I stared at the beach, at the place where the water
turned into the shore. It kept shifting.
I stared so long at the water it didn't look wet anymore.
I waited so long to be saved
I forgot what I was being saved for.
Why I was waving my hands.
Sometimes I thought I loved the island.
I ate some sand.
I kissed the land like a man saved.
I remembered a story about a man who ate an airplane.
Sometimes things washed up on the shore.
An umbrella. A crate.
Everything that arrived I partially ate.
Sometimes things washed up
that were invented while I was on the island.
Cloud-shaped things.
I waited for someone to invent an inflatable airplane.

Once I think I saw a plane
but I had forgotten what planes looked like
and what they were for.
Sometimes when I'd think about being saved
I wondered if I'd ever miss the island,
when I was miles away from the island.
When I could no longer kiss the island.
Now I sometimes wonder if I ever
made it off the island.

III.

NEAR-LIFE EXPERIENCE

Weird. I almost died. Don't touch
my pivot point, my cicatrix—

it prickles me. My center
of gravity, my weak spot

for mortality. Where they held me
when I got dipped.

If you think about it
you can figure out

what groups of animals are called:
a smear of snails, a misery

of pigeons. I almost slipped
on this almost bird, fallen

to the earth like a ruined,
a baby-blue breakfast.

"Abundant sunshine." The mica sparkles
through him/her/it.

POEM WITH A THREAT

Columning storm cloud, natch, dead bird.
My fear of X is worse than X,

more scary. What am I wearing?
The less I recognize myself, the less

I contradict—scratch, feel contrary
to my mirror image in the "pool of grief"

down there. No one would ever say that.
But I might say "puddle of despair."

OF A LONELY SEASON

I scarce can take it in—
I think she speaks

of supersaturation.
The satisfaction in winter,

then: not its having dwindled,
but confirming I had reason

to dread. And the appley smell
on this side of the pond, still—if only

by associative memory; ducks
with their pretty heads.

They just stand there on the ice
of snow. Are they frozen down?

The earworm of insomnia
comes back like a theme. Laughter

as a kind of signaling
that one gets it.

My friends are amazing.
They, like, float—buoyed up

by my despairing. *You don't know
how much you mean to me,*

one wrote in a book,
instead of telling me.

WALKS ARE USELESS II

There's nothing to be sad about.
My sadness grows restless, nostalgic

for a better bore, the tragic bore
of yesteryear. The stink of the city

grows worse, but at the same rate
that we get used to it. 'Tis a bore

and nothing more. Even the clouds
are bored, arrange themselves into more

and more exotic vegetables.
Where is the war? I can't see it.

I feel incredible. What I mean is,
I feel like no one would believe me.

WALKS ARE USELESS III

After reading a bit of Kafka's diary, I go out
to check the status of this century's clouds.

If they were meaningless
then, are they less so now?

I sweep my arm through the air, and it leaves
no trace, no neon zee. I seem

continuous. The view from nowhere
says I'm tiny, and stuck

in the approximate present.
It's not even speaking directly to me.

And then a blind man says,
When you're blind,

you don't see black,
you just don't see.

POEM WITH DIORAMA

What are you looking at, dog.
OK, I don't belong in the park,

with nature: I'm not enough rich,
not enough poor; the fluff from a tree

makes my heart sore. I'm not crazy.
I just prefer the feminine remove

of a reproduction, of a living room—
the miniature texts exquisitely real,

if you had the means to read them.
Tiny poison in the wallpaper

in theory would eventually kill you.
Did you know fruit flies can have sex

for twenty minutes? That's like half
their lifespan. There's a couple going at it

on the parquet floor. The future
of the species depends on it. Unless

they're just writhing in death throes—
hard to tell at this size. Either way

I'm not traumatized.

ELEGY AT CHESTNUT AND RIVER

Squirrel in the road, squashed
to an outline of itself: cute,
even in death. I can't miss it

if I never knew it. Can I?
If I pick it up, it will weigh
either more or less

than I expect. Will smear
a little blood on my fingers.
It will smell rich.

It's a squirrel: not
looking for a monument
or a headstone. It wants

to be left on the street,
the spot where it was last
alive, stuck in the running-

across shape. It wants to keep
running forever, but
it can't stop stopping.

POEM WITH A PLOT

It starts off good, with this woman
who keeps on forgetting her name. Turns out

it's all about a magical monkey.
I wish most days didn't end up that way—

like episodes of a realist sitcom
where problems aren't solved so much

as abandoned, if not flat ruined.
My emotions are all set to default.

If I do enough things I hate in one day
I might learn something ... or just feel

generally stubbed. Where my soul
was. The claim is "Some bunny loves me."

It doesn't say unconditionally.

MY ENEMY

has fallen in love with me. A finger gun cocked

in the small of my back, his other hand
around my neck, he whispers, *Quoi, quoi, quoi.* . . .

His fingers smell like bowstrings, breath
like milk. Is this from my dream? I fantasize

to my rape fantasy, but I can't get closer
than this. My skin feels pinched. I drive

down the street and there is something
under every leaf; each flutters independently

as if to its own breeze. Again that silky breath,
its omnipresenceness. . . . The party isn't over

but he's made a French exit—he wants me
wanting more, and I want it too—these quantities,

our needless desires. We require promises
to lay out like pinafores, white eyelet dresses.

To snap like tiny needles, along gossamer
stress fractures. Fault lines. Sweetness.

We succumb to this. A random symphony
of car alarms accompanies his kiss.

POEM WITHOUT AN EPIGRAPH

It's going to be another bad winter,
as in, not a good example of winter:

you can sit on the beach in November
with no coat. If a dog wants to play,

why not throw your phone
into the ocean? It probably floats;

it's mostly plastic. Earphones
too—the sand here "sings."

This would be a good spot
for a stand selling single-use

remote-control boats—robots
as far as the eye can see.

Let's ruin the world
and get it over with. I hate

"the sea." Except as a vessel
for my message in a bottle—

what good would it be?
My heat-seeking missive

in seawater ink, the faintest
blue, coasts, disappearing

horizonward. It could be for anyone.
But aims for you.

SCREENSHOT FOR ALLEN

Here's you. Here's your street. Now zoom out—way out.
That speck on the right-hand side by the scrollbar is me.

Hanging on the coast. Hiking around, in the cold-day air,
cerulean wind whipping at our faces with our own hair.

Over the dunes, always more dunes. You would have said,
Why does it have to be so sandy? Since you weren't there,

I said it instead. I wonder what you were doing then.
Probably writing out equations on unlined paper

in your fast loopy hand—something I couldn't comment on
except at this superficial level. How stupid of me

to find your pencil marks sexy. To prefer them
to the world: the huge freezing ocean: it does nothing

for me. This gull wing jutting up out of the sand.
Is there a bird down there, objecting? Politely?

Excuse me, world. I wasn't ready to be buried.

EGO OF THE DISTANCE

Mysteried distance, resistant distance: it glimmers
out of visibility. The distance that runs seamingly

along all my images like a fold. Like a hairline
crack down my mirror—I am always

looking at the distance, at it splitting me.
I am warped along that fault.

Sometimes the distance looks at me
and for a moment I feel requited

but then the distance rushes away
at impossible speeds like the other side

of the balloon, the other end
of the expanding universe. It doesn't remember

when we were touching, eye to eye.
Or just doesn't fetishize that time like I do.

I call out after the distance, *Is it me?* The distance
responds with Doppler effect, *It's meeeeee*

POEM WITH A SNOWMAN

You must think of the thing
to regard it, and this ruins the effect:
thing absorbs your gaze; the heat

transfer from your brain waves excites,
starts to melt it like a wicked queen.
See the ice trees shimmer and drip

as they shrink. See the forest level sink
as its new form is shunted invisibly up
to the sun. Photosynthesis in reverse:

it makes a creepy sound like a suction cup
pulled off a mirror. Try to do this
without watching yourself do it

in the background. Impossible—
the mirror always knows. Think *nothing*
and you're still not thinking nothing.

POEM WITH NEGATION

I run not away, but untoward—
through the malaise of a Tuesday,

past the man in the shirt
that says HAVE A KNIFE DAY,

the men in fatigues.
They float out 3-D.

Coffee cup. Dog shit. Dog shit.
The ice-cream-truck horror theme.

Past the cracked door, the possible act
of good will. Toward the definition,

untoward the meaning. I run
through the emphases—

It doesn't mean anything.
It *doesn't* mean anything.

It doesn't *mean* anything.
It doesn't mean *anything*.

POEM WITHOUT FREE WILL

Scatterplot of insect parts,
needle over E, karaoke

scansion of the radio,
I want my anachronism back—

his head in the rearview mirror,
double-bass voice extrinsic

like running commentary
and now I hate this movie,

I'd rather watch the wind-
shield—at least the wind

is approaching.
Time doesn't just fly;

it ninja-stars me.
It's obvious to want to die,

but in the poem, I have to.
No life but in desire.

NO NEW YEARS JUST HIGHER NUMBERS

I guess I'm still drunk, throwing rocks
out onto the iced-over pond.

You feel old. Your words make smoke.
Yesterday I watched the sun set

from a plane. My past disappears
like that, with grandiose fanfare

out of proportion to the event.
Where will I be in a year

is beside the point to this
stillness, the waiting to fall through.

How much I love you.
Is beside the point to the descent.

The clouds feel like nothing
when you're in them.

If this were an elevator dream
I'd suggest we hold our breath

or our arms up maybe,
make ourselves lighter.

THE WORD *FUSEKI*

In that I think of my brother,
his serious face while gaming—

the serious frown, crook between
his caterpillar eyebrows—

and then Allen, the counterintuitive
move—"It's not 'interesting'!"—

getting up to fuck around
on the marimba,

Charlie Brown and Debussy.
I now hate the word *interesting*.

In that I once tied my brother at chess;
in that it's not called a "tie." The word

endgame. In that I almost won
at ping-pong, then Robinson asked him

why he was playing left-handed.
The word *cannot*, in that my brother,

asked to use the word *cannot* in a sentence,
wrote: "I don't like cannots."

(I wanted to keep that.
Why did I give it away?)

In that I now hate San Francisco.
There are no good bars in San Francisco,

just a microclimate hovering around you
through the fog, a little cloud of heat.

You drink your warm, turned wine
and hold your ground in the fight

and then you cry outside
in the scumbag street.

In that I miss my erased memory
of San Francisco—smudged over,

my pentimento memory—
we burned the edges off a map

to "antique" it, found a lighter
and haloed the rim—

and my brother. In that
I always say *my brother.*

(If he's mine,
why can't I keep him?)

Notes on the poems:

The poems in Section II were composed as part of a poem-a-day project in April of 2005 and originally appeared on Chris Tonelli's blog, The Steinach Operation.

"Disasterpoem (for KR)" is for Kathleen Rooney.

"Poem with a Threat" was partially inspired by a post on Jonathan Mayhew's blog, ¡Bemsha Swing!

The first line of "Of a Lonely Season" is from "Epilogue: Epithalamion" by Kathleen Rooney.

"Walks Are Useless II" is after Chris Tonelli.

"Poem with a Plot" makes reference to a short story called "A Shinagawa Monkey" by Haruki Murakami.

"Poem Without an Epigraph" is for Chris Nealon.

"Screenshot for Allen" is for Allen Lee.

"Poem with a Snowman" is after Wallace Stevens.

"No New Years Just Higher Numbers" is for John Cotter.

"The Word *Fuseki*" is for Adam Gabbert.

Photo by Michael Gabbert

Elisa Gabbert is the author of the chap-
books *Thanks for Sending the Engine* and *My
Fear of X* (both from Kitchen Press), and,
with Kathleen Rooney, three collaborative
works: *Something Really Wonderful* (Dancing
Girl Press), *That Tiny Insane Voluptuousness*
(Otoliths), and *Don't ever stay the same; keep
changing* (Spooky Girlfriend Press). She is the
poetry editor of *Absent* and currently works
at a software startup in Boston. She blogs at
http://thefrenchexit.blogspot.com.